Song of Spring

Fong Fong

Print information available on the last page.

Rev. date: 06/07/2016

To order additional copies of this book, contact:
Xlibris
1-888-795-4274
www.Xlibris.com
Orders@Xlibris.com

Song of Spring 春之歌

for Violin and Piano

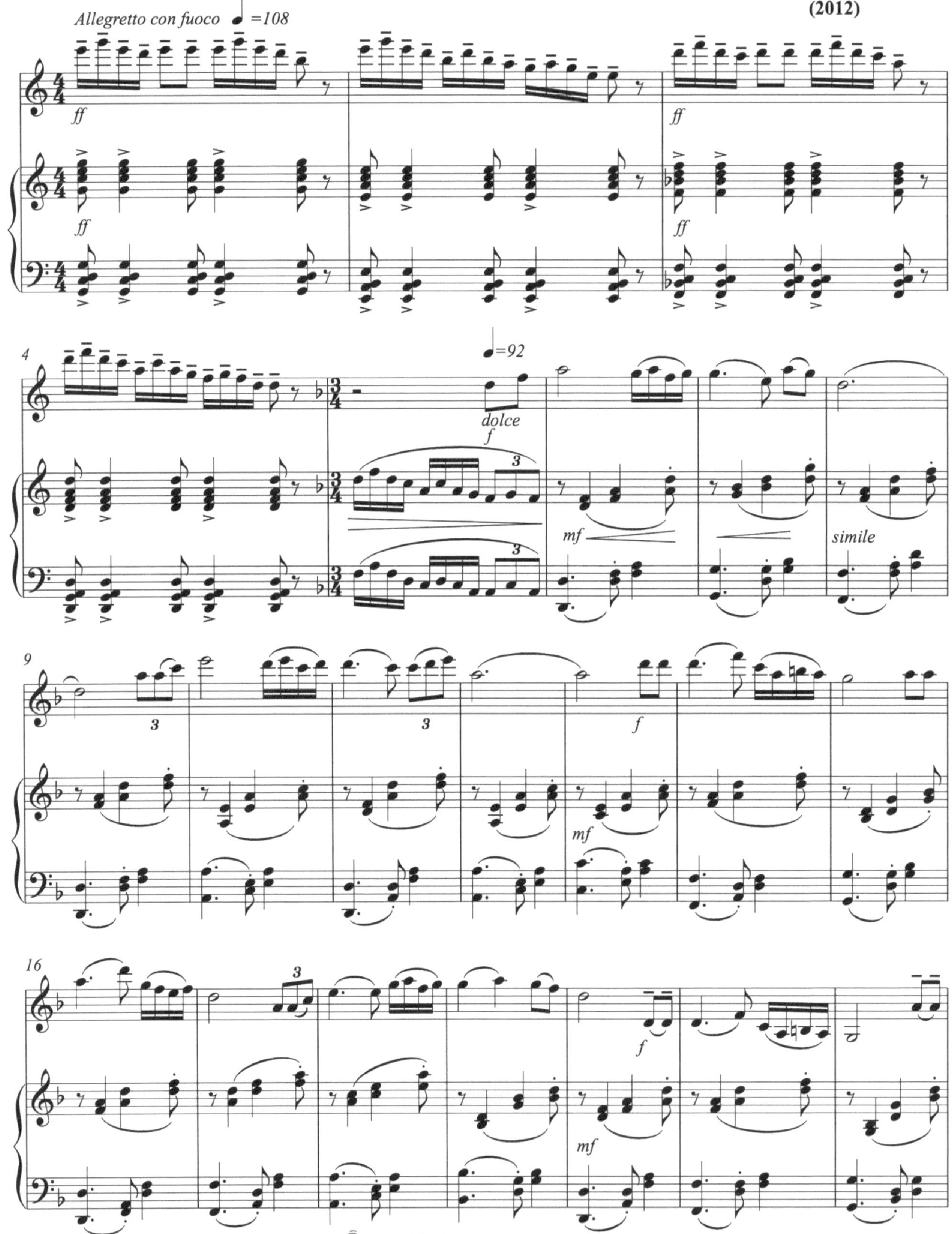

Full Score

Fong Fong 方放
(2012)

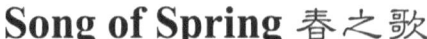

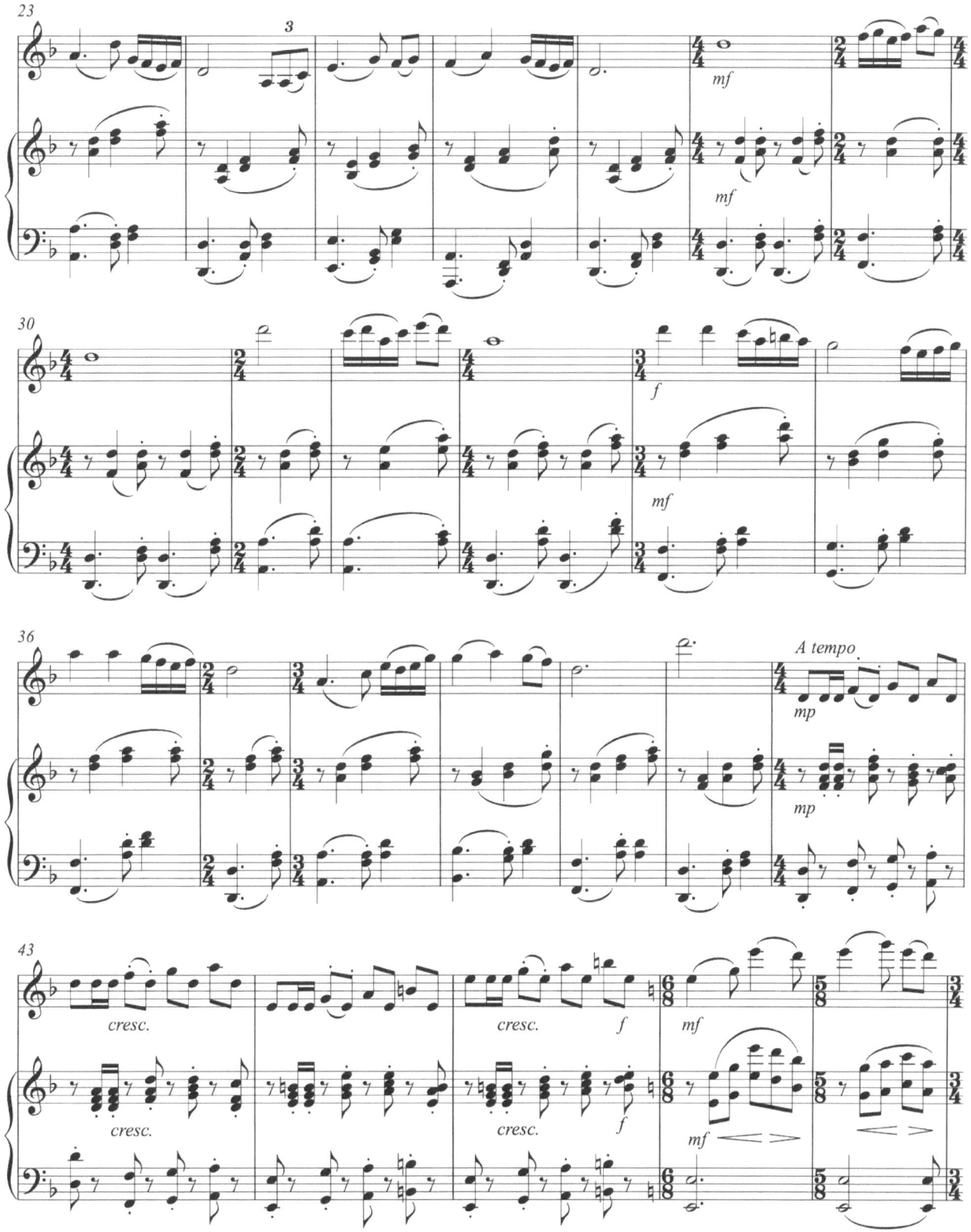

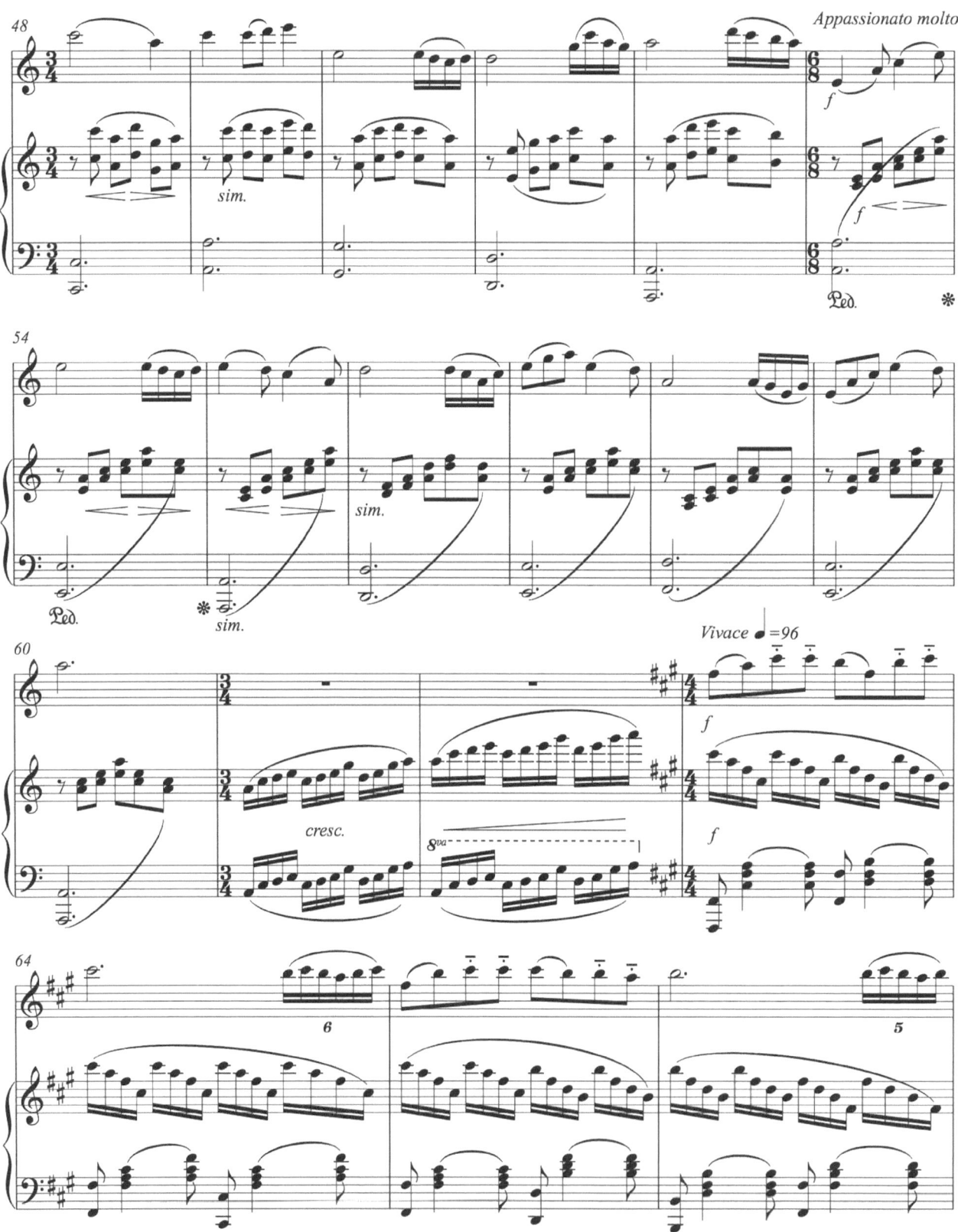

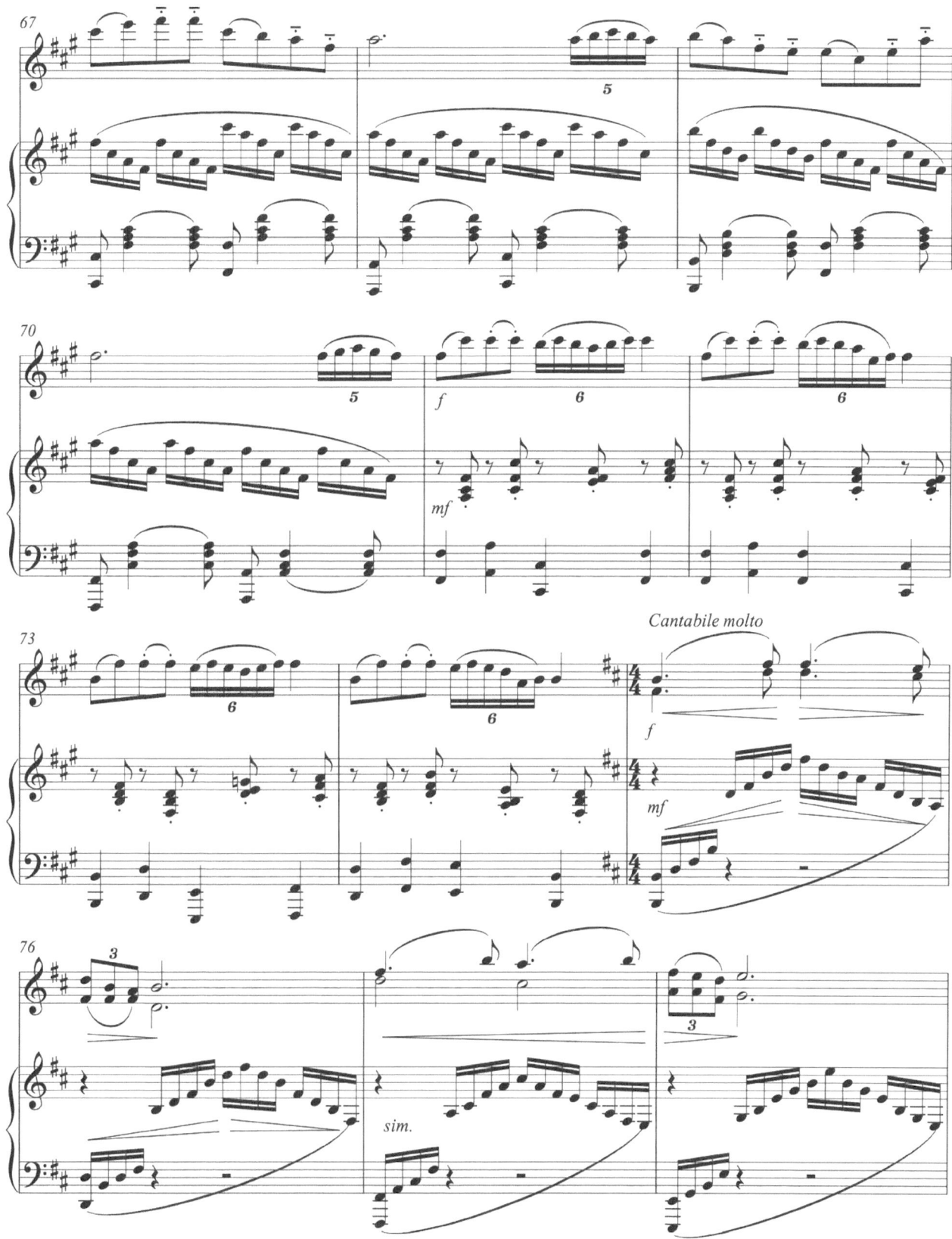

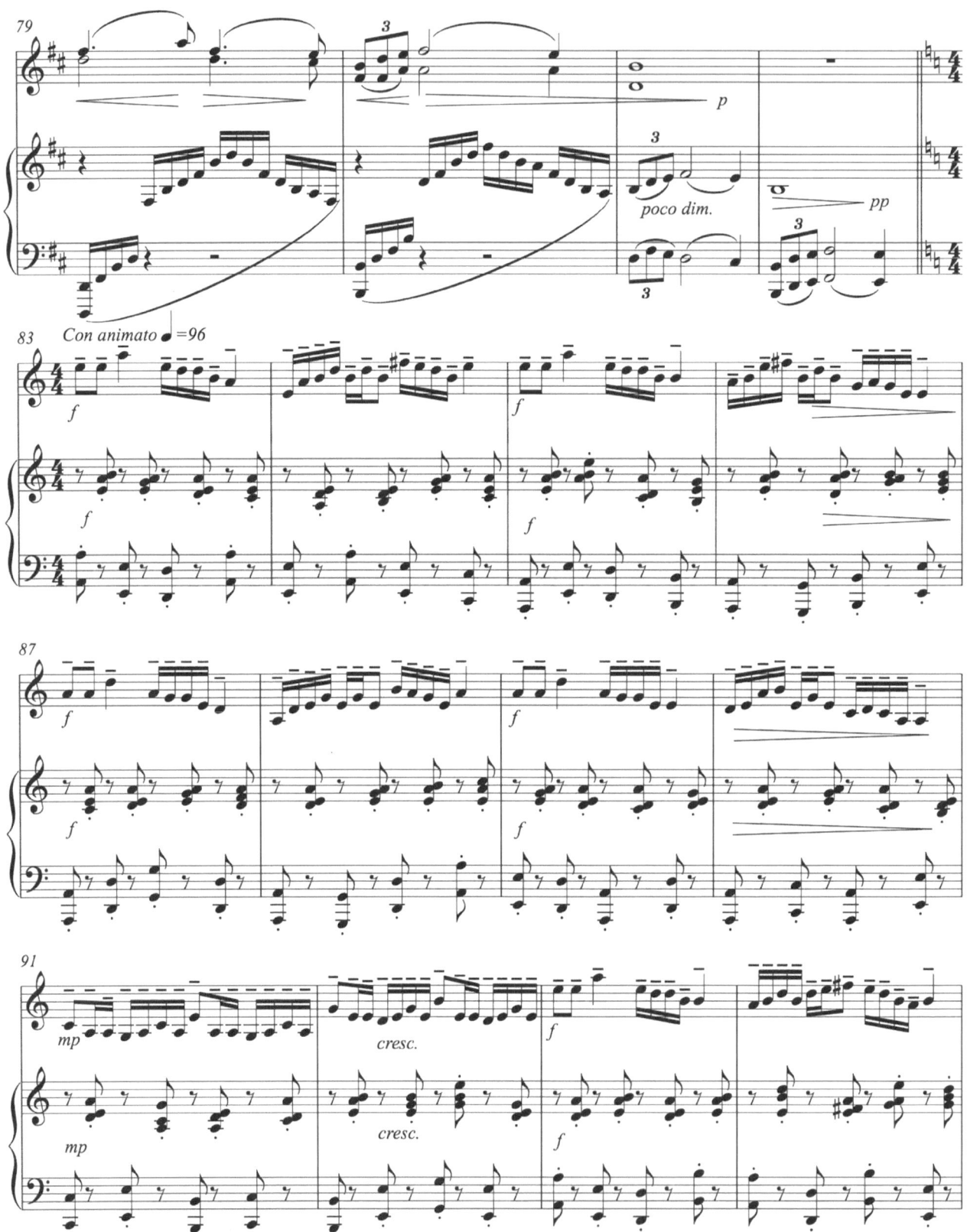

5

6

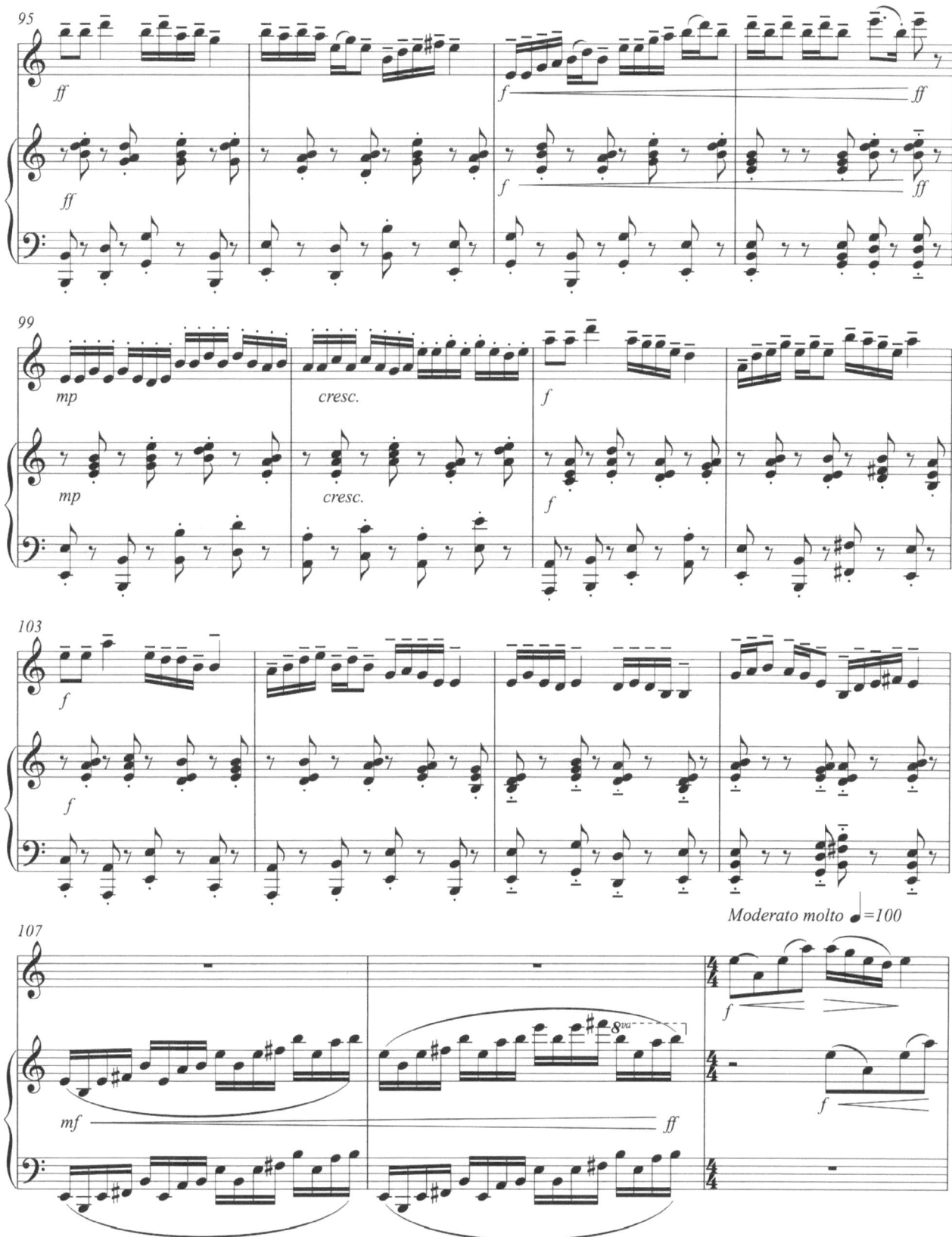

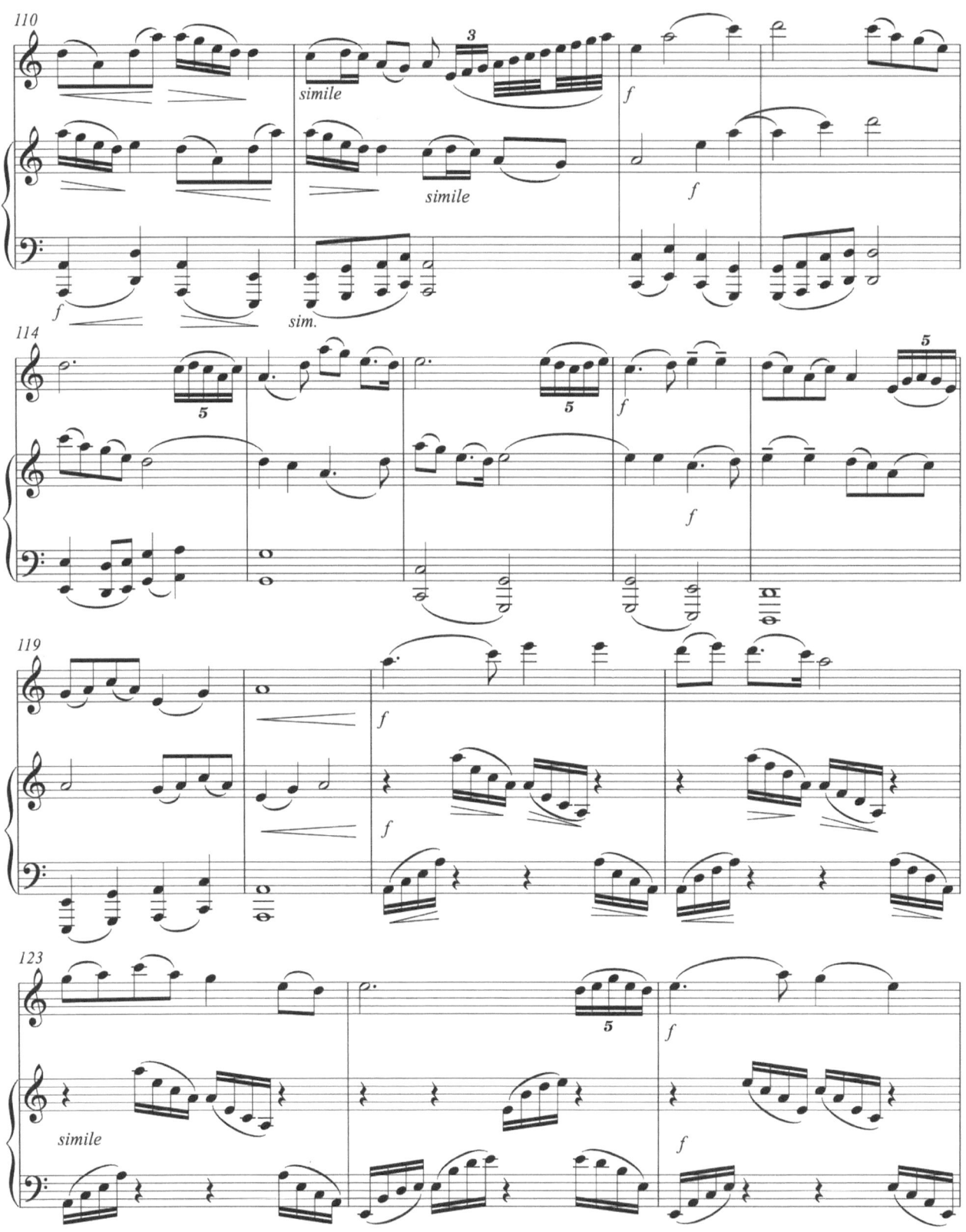

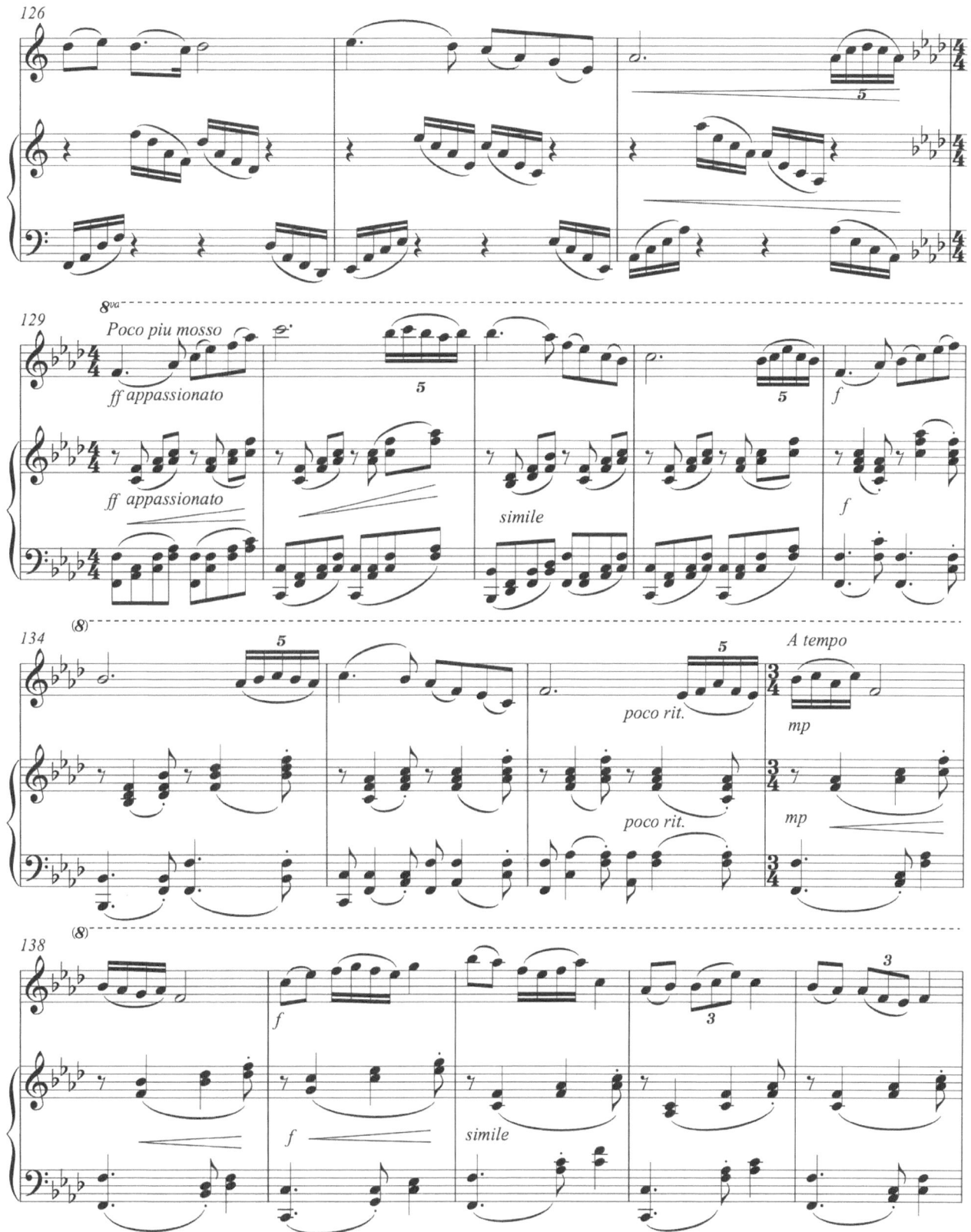

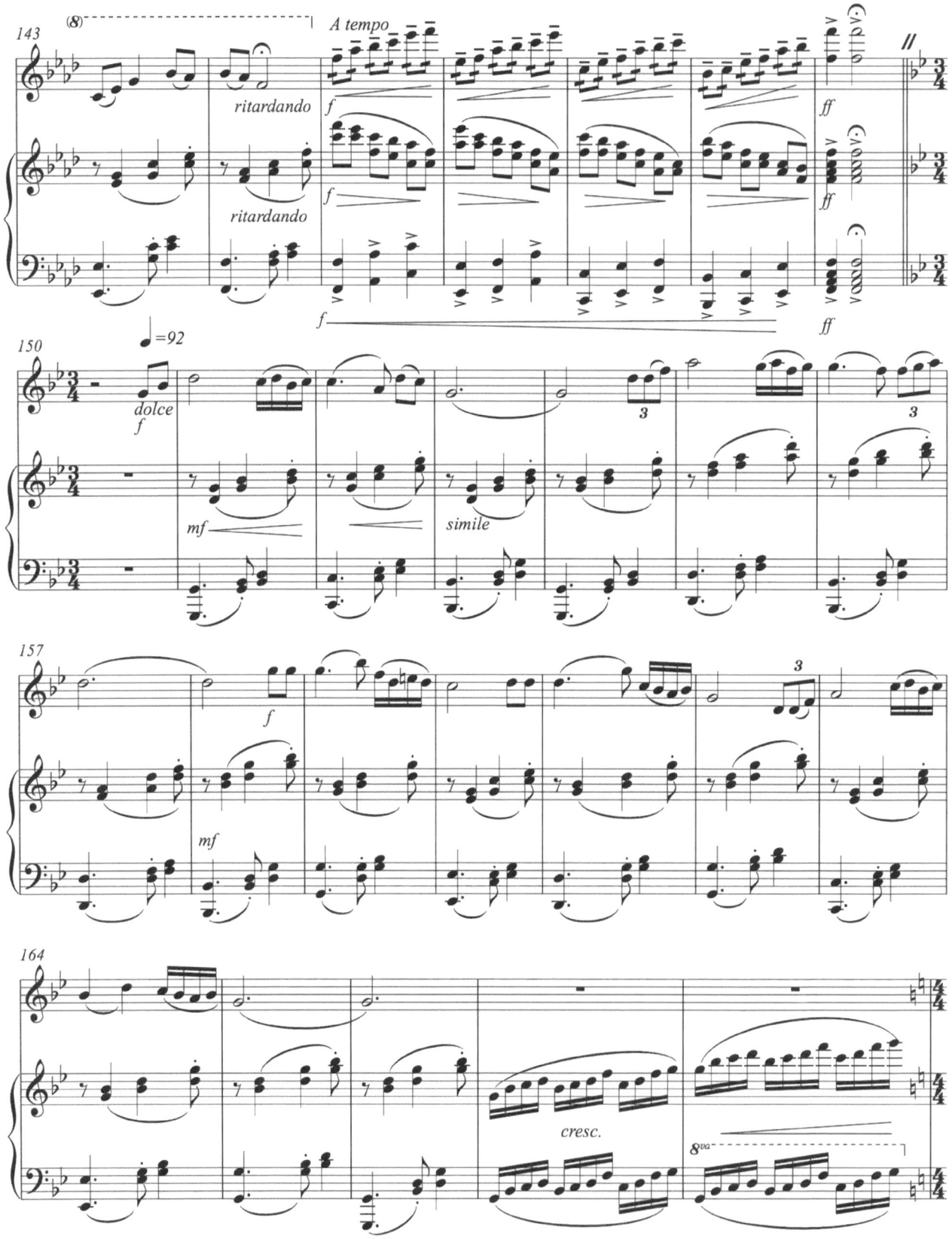

10

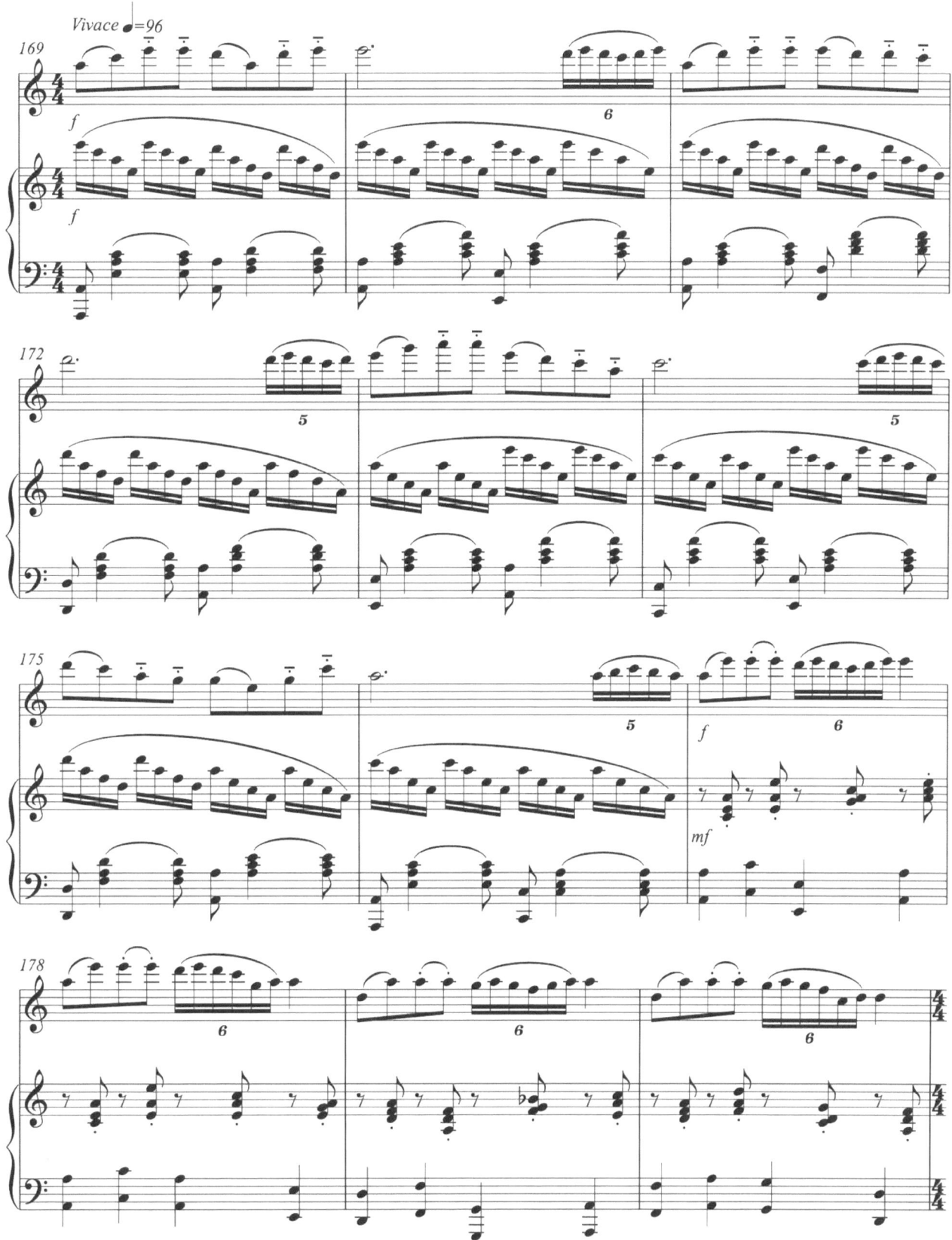

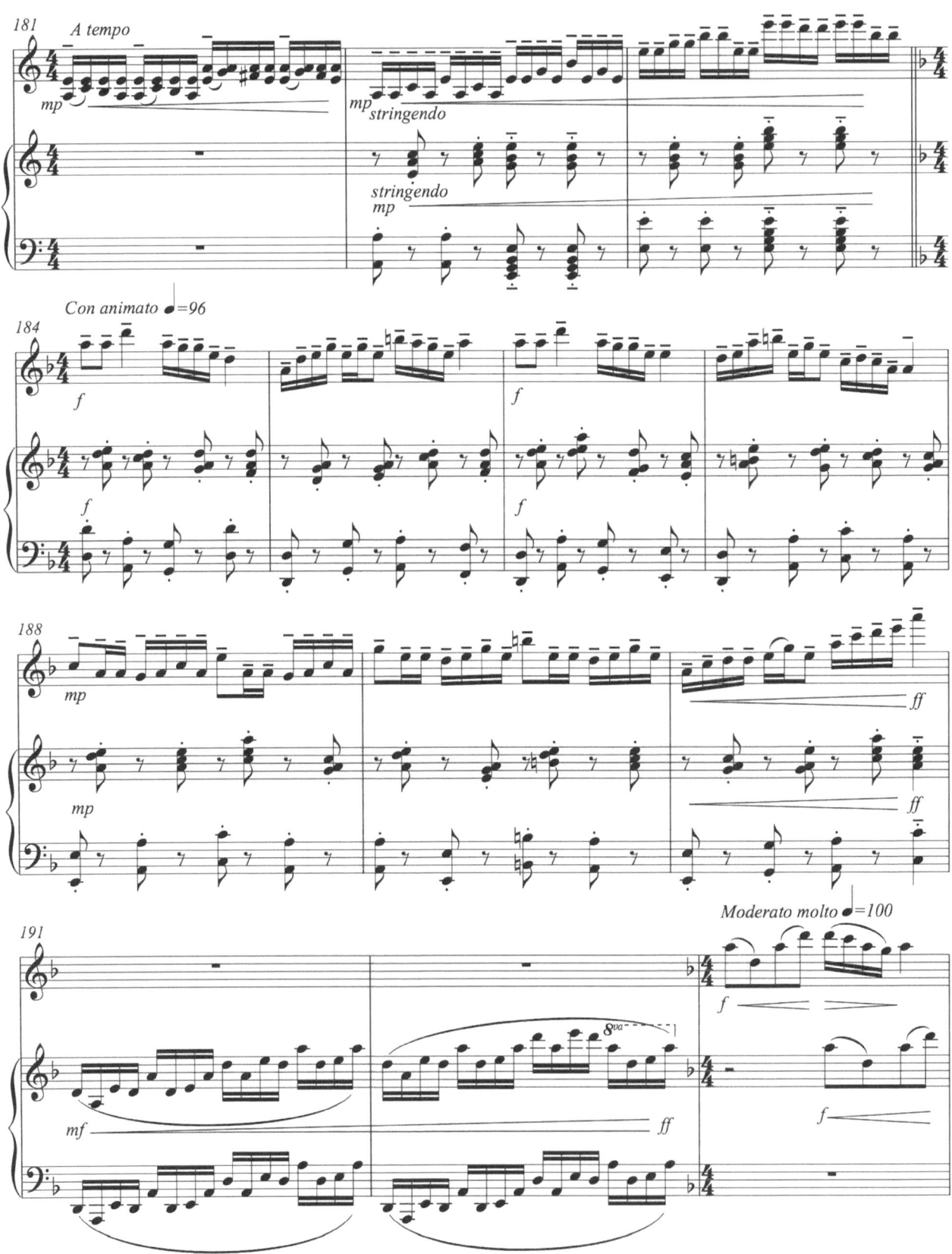

12

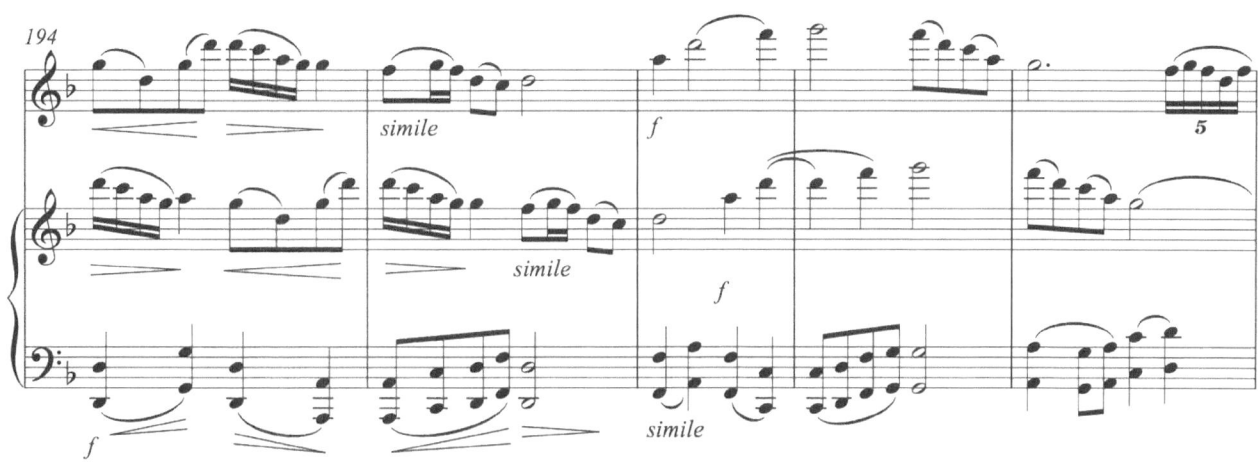

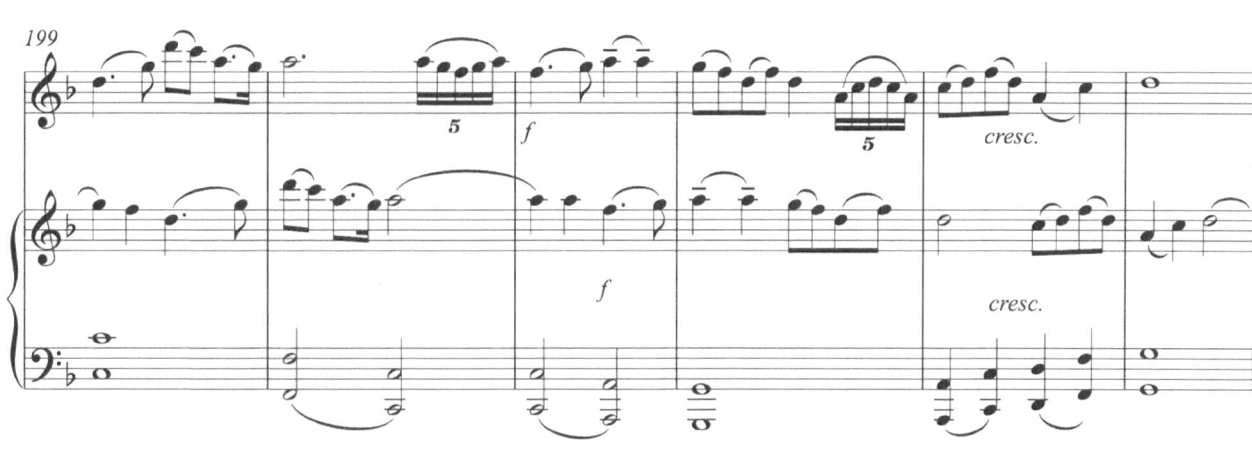

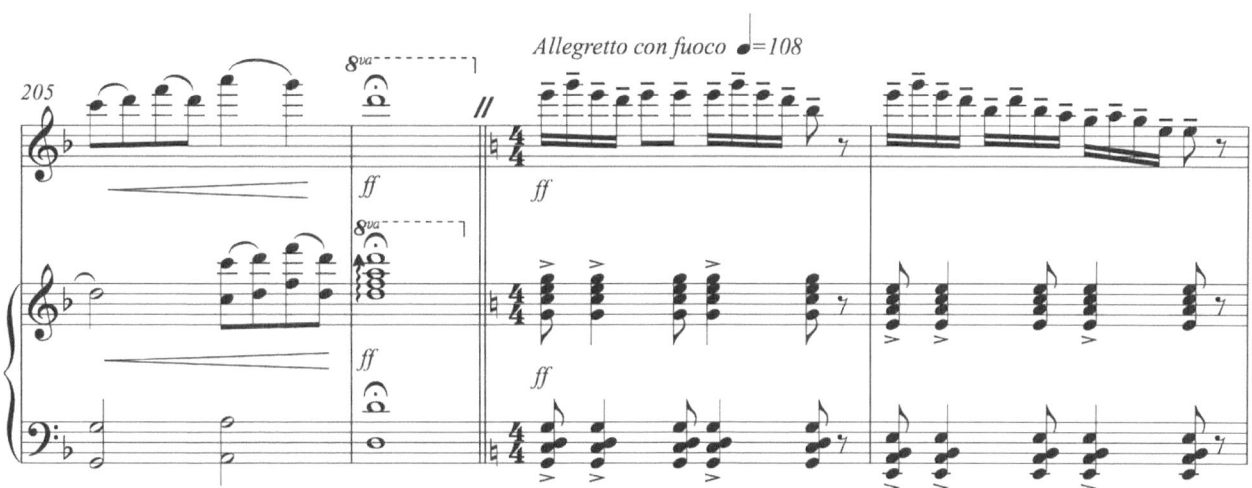

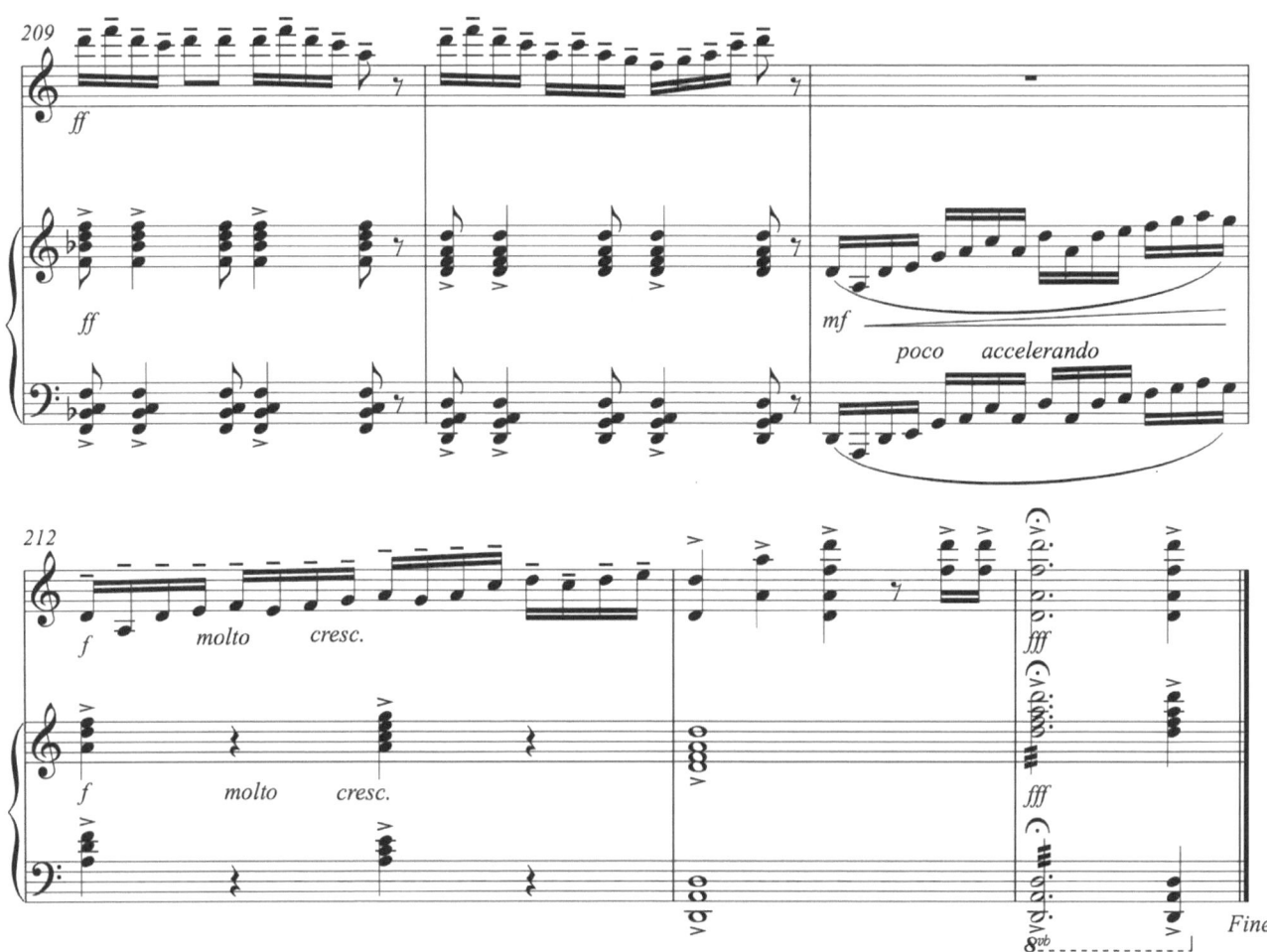

Fine

Violin

Song of Spring 春之歌
for Violin and Piano

Fong Fong 方放
(2012)

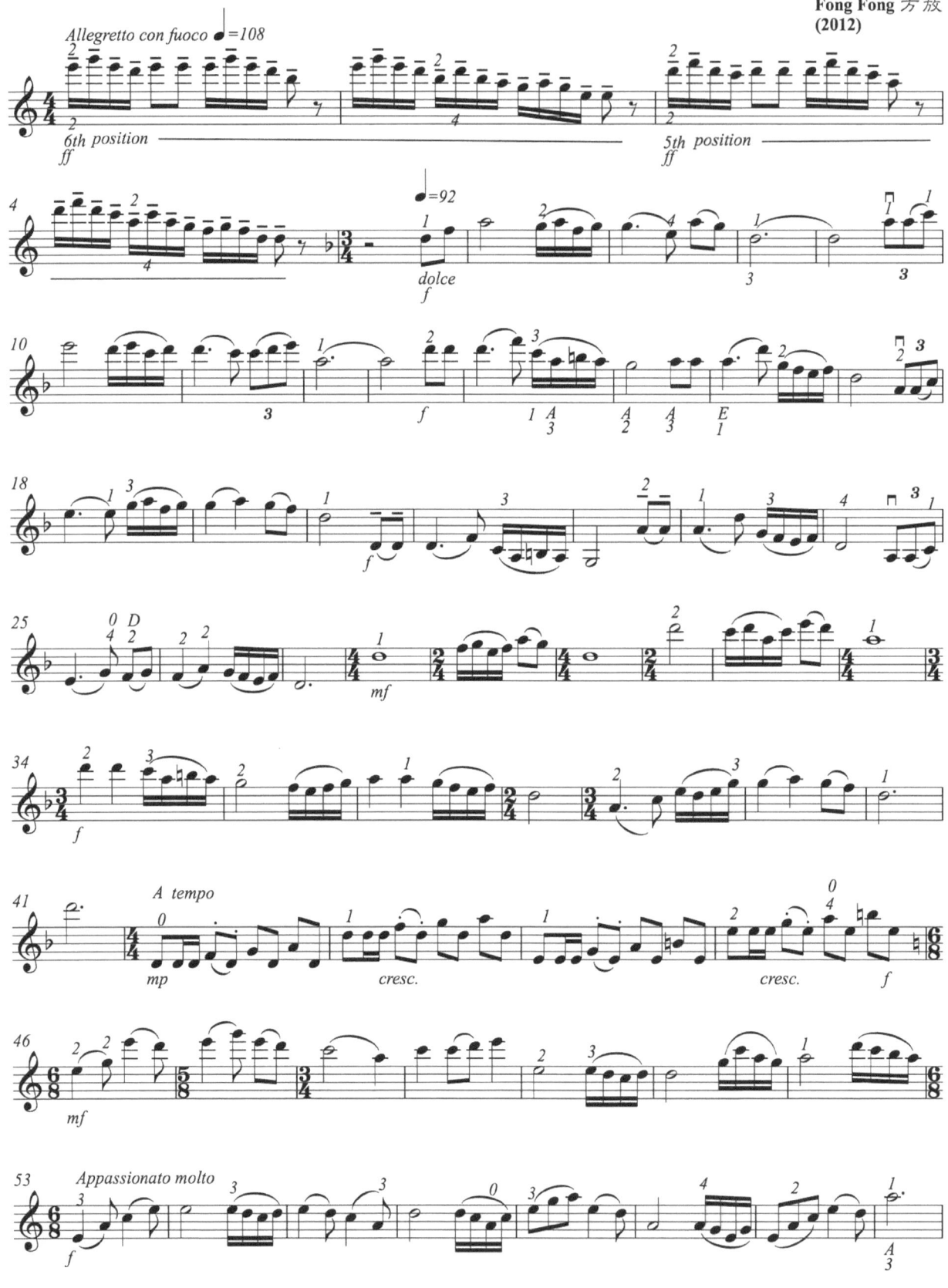

2

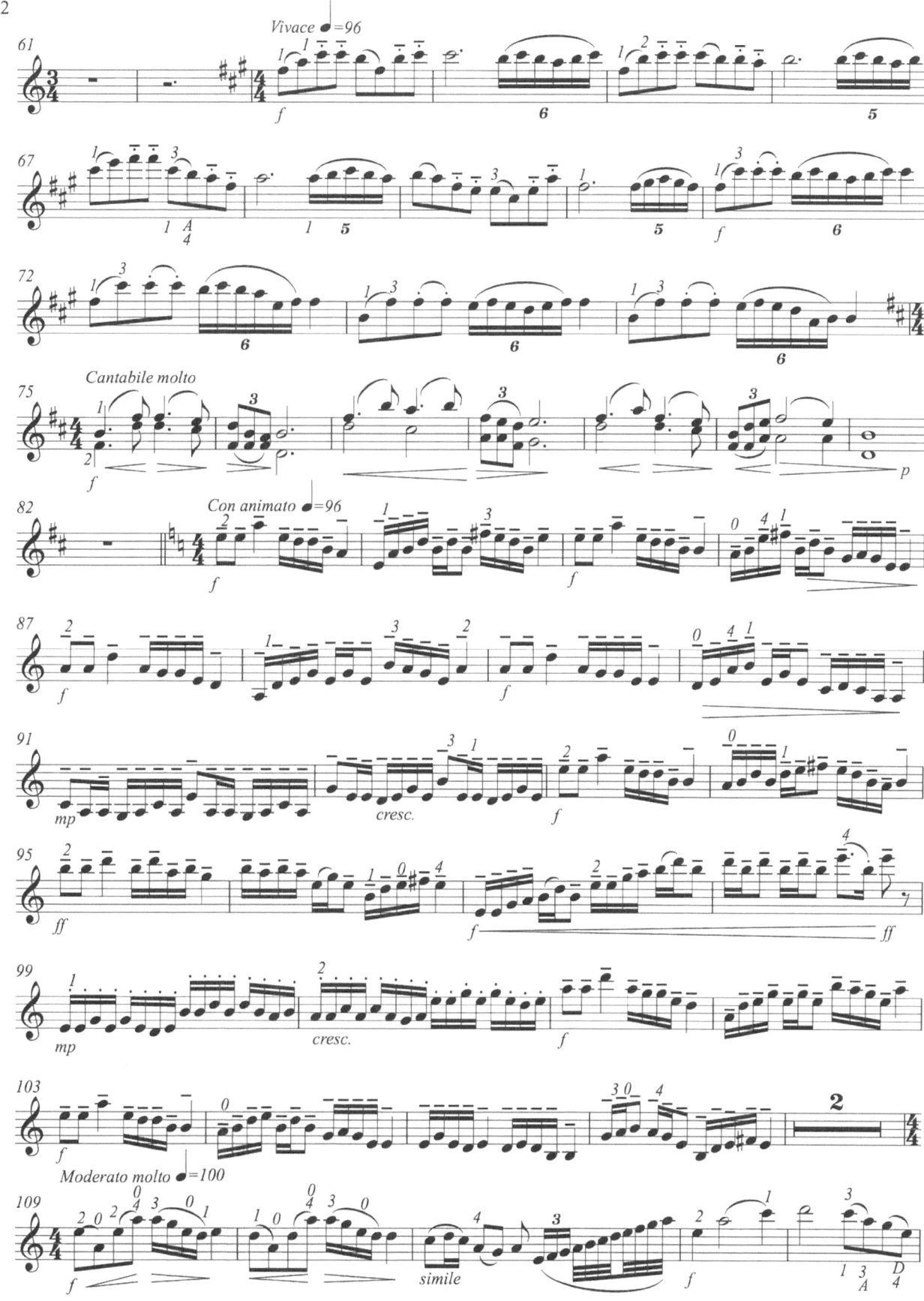

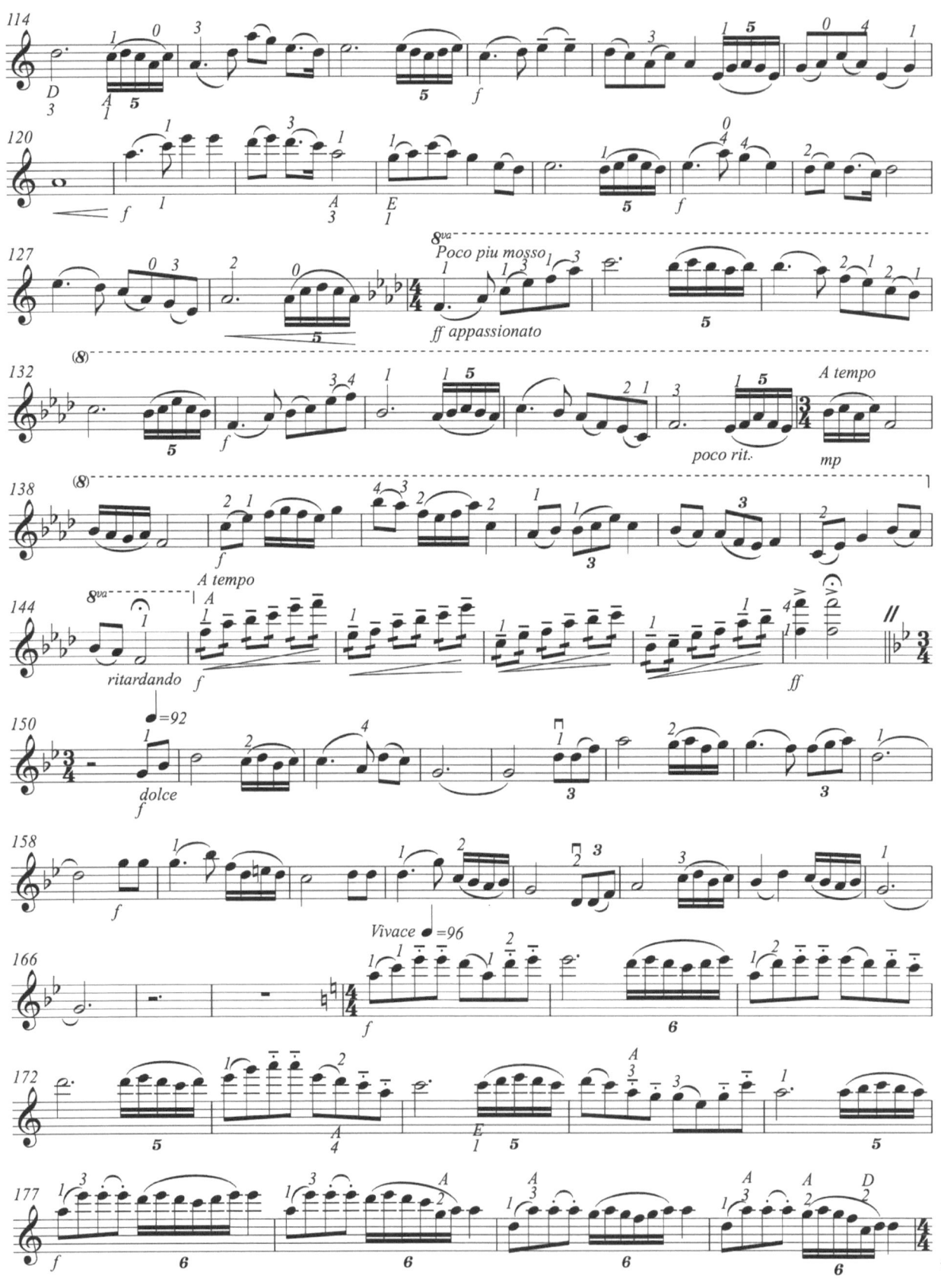

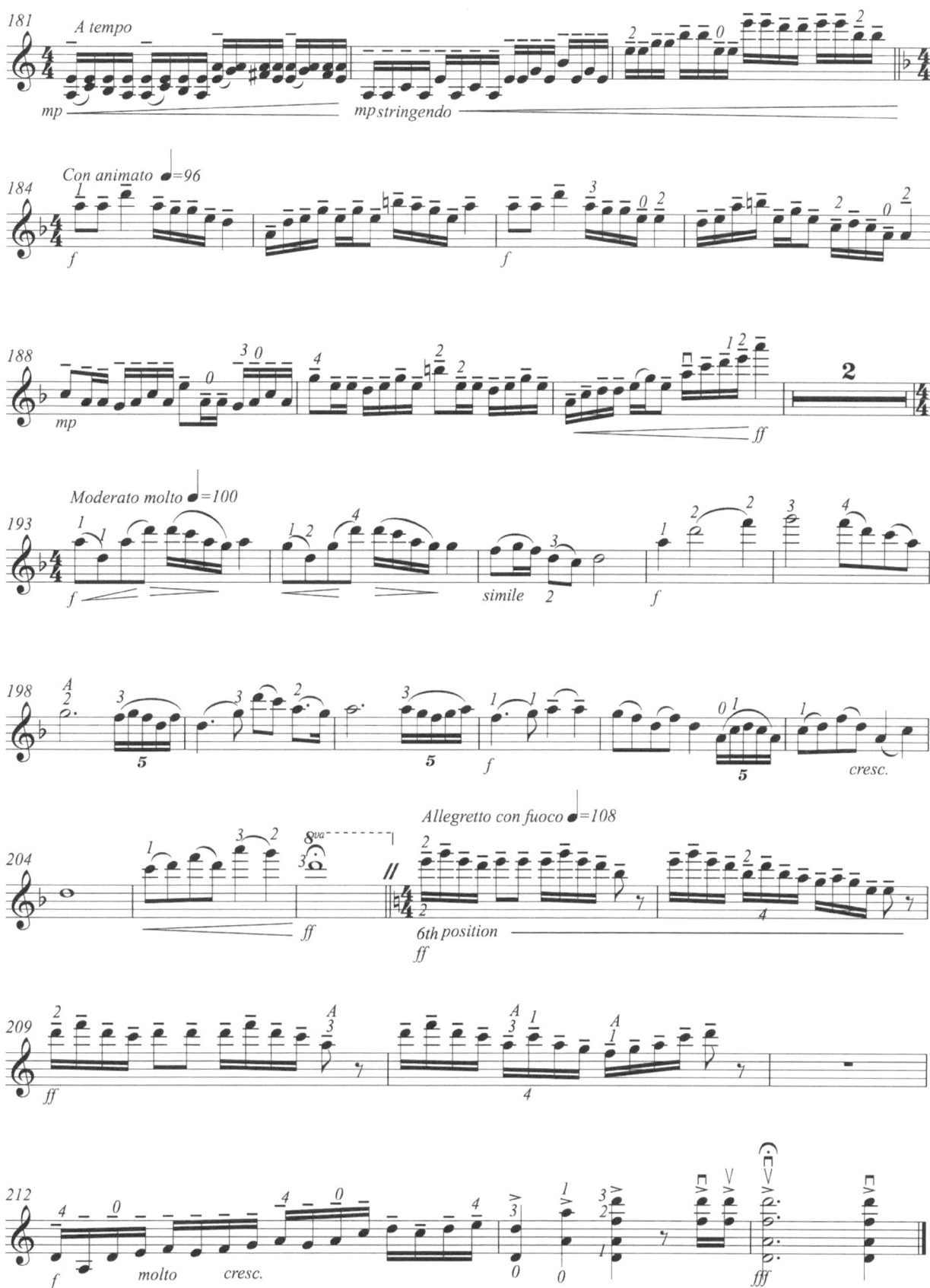